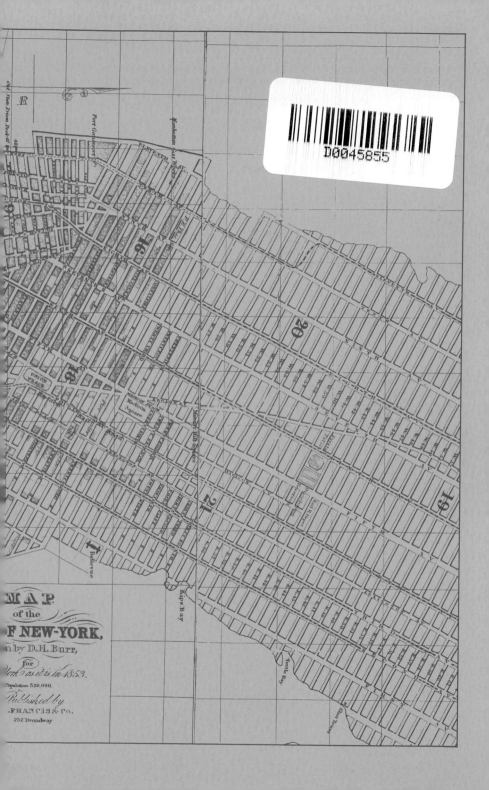

MAP.

of the

F NEW-YORK,

by D.H. Burr,

for

ork as it is in 1853.

Population 520,000.

Published by

FRANCIS & Co.

252 Broadway

Letters to Phil

Gene Schermerhorn

Letters to Phil
Memories of a
New York Boyhood,
1848~1856

with thirty~four drawings
by the author

Foreword by Brendan Gill

A Leslie Dwinell Book
New York Bound/New York
1982

My warmest thanks go to

the late Julia Diamant Wolfman;

Leslie Dwinell, for directing every phase of the publishing process with professional skill, equanimity, and a fine-tuned sense of humor;

Dr. Larry Sullivan of the New York Historical Society and Eric M. Kampmann, for the help and encouragement I received during the preparation of this book;

my husband, Myron, for his unflagging support and understanding which sustained me from initial idea to project's completion.

Barbara L. Cohen
Publisher

Copyright © 1982 by New York Bound.

A Leslie Dwinell Book.
First published in 1982 by New York Bound, 43 West 54th Street, New York, NY 10019.

82-060414

ISBN 0-9608788-0-7   Distributed by Kampmann & Company

First Edition

End papers: Map of the City of New York, drawn by D.H. Burr for *New York As It Is in 1853* (population, 520,000), published by C.S. Francis and Company, 252 Broadway.

Printed in the United States of America.

10 9 8 7 6 5 4 3 2 1

Designed by Parallelogram/Marsha Cohen

Contents

Illustrations

Foreword by Brendan Gill

Every scrap of the past is worth preserving, and not least for this reason: that from one generation to the next we can never be certain whether the value of a given object—a coin, a book, a bundle of old letters—is great or small. Nor is this inconsistency in respect to value a function of anything as simple as scarcity; it is related also to how remarkably often scholars are capable of changing their minds. History is a speculation based on a vast kitchen-midden of indiscriminate facts, from which a variety of contradictory hypotheses can be plucked. We destroy at our peril what strikes us today as trash, for tomorrow we may be damned for having failed to detect its obvious importance.

I am myself the proprietor of a veritable compost-heap of family records, which find their way to me seemingly without my intending them to do so. Among my favorite memorabilia are those that bear witness to astonishing leaps through time, made possible in most cases by exceptional longevity. Himalaya-like peaks of paper rise from the buried surface of my desk; half-way up one of the peaks, I encounter the first page of an unpublished manuscript—the autobiography of my grand-aunt, Emma Jane Bowen. It begins, "A little over a hundred years ago, when I was being held aloft at my christening. . . ." Aunt Emma was born during the Civil War, the last child of her father's late second marriage. He, Patrick Bowen—my great-grandfather—had been born in the eighteenth century and she told many stories about him to my grandchildren, who can be expected to live well on into the twenty-first century.

A similar span of time is encompassed by my friend Ned Perkins. He and I are members of the Century Club, in New York City, and one afternoon in 1976 the group of men with whom we were sitting in the clubhouse began to discuss the Bicentennial celebrations that were then getting under way. Somebody mentioned that while we were fortunate to have the documents written by the Founding Fathers, how much more fortunate we would be if only we could hear their voices as well—an advantage that, thanks to recordings, will be in future an ever-increasing commonplace. After a silence, Ned said, "I have heard an eighteenth-century voice." We pressed him to tell us how that was possible. "I was born in 1883," he said, "and I was brought up in part by my great-grandmother, who as a little girl was taken down to the new Federal Hall, on Wall Street, to observe Washington being sworn in as the first President of the United States. That was in 1790."

Ned Perkins will be one hundred years old next spring; by now, he has lived a year or so longer than his beloved great-grandmother did. Seated in a favorite chair in a garden on the slopes of the Tyringham valley, in the Berkshires of western Massachusetts, he tells his great-grandchildren the story of his great-grandmother's having clambered up onto her father's shoulders in order to get the best possible view of General Washington. Ned has a lively sense of how, between the two of them, his great-grandmother and he have contrived to link eight generations of the family, scattered over four centuries.

Voices are perhaps the most precious souvenirs of the past that we inherit; after voices come diaries and letters, which, if they are well-written, with unselfconscious fidelity echo the voice of the writer. The letters in this book possess that merit in full measure; we are indeed lucky to have them. They bring a lost New York to life; we hug it to us and will never let it go.

ix

Introduction

Once there was a city where nothing stayed still. People, street traffic, industry, ideas, the pulse of life itself seemed to move faster and be more intense than anywhere else. People came and went—worked, prospered, failed, whatever they did—on a grand scale. People and things changed from day to day, it seemed. Buildings came into existence apparently overnight, one by one at first and then whole blocks of them. Some neighborhoods went from elegant to shabby, while others, never before considered livable by the gentry, became fashionable within the space of a few years. This was the city of New York in the nineteenth century.

New York was home to Edward Eugene Schermerhorn throughout his life. He had particularly strong and affectionate memories of his boyhood during the 1840s and 1850s, and he set them down, starting in 1886, in a series of ten illustrated letters to his young nephew, Phil. In a note preceding the first of the letters, Uncle Gene explains to Phil, "I propose to write for you some things which I can remember about New York when I was a boy . . . to amuse you at present . . . and to interest you when you are older and can appreciate the great changes that have taken place."

Gene did indeed see great changes, for during that period, New York made the transition from an outsize town to a complex, cosmopolitan city. By the time he writes down his memories in the 1880s, New York has become an international capital. So it remains today, though again, so many changes have taken place that for us, reading Gene's letters, there is the feeling of traveling in a time machine. This introduction is in the nature of a time-machine road-map, intended to give the reader the context that Gene assumes without stating—a sense of place, time, and history, as well as their relationship to our own time.

I

While *Letters to Phil* focuses on the nineteenth century and reverberates into the twentieth, we would do well to remember that the entire history of New York is one of almost continual change. Start with the earliest accounts of the terrain: There were sparkling streams and thick woodlands filled with an abundance of vegetation, fish, and animals—a veritable Eden. Now, of course, this wilderness is gone, but even more telling to the history of change in New York is the fact that the very contours of the land have changed. Rocky hills have been leveled; streams and ponds (including the ones where young Gene Schermerhorn would skate) have been filled in; new land has been created by adding landfill onto the coastline, pushing New York farther out into the sea. But no one official set out to change the topography of New York. All this was incidental to the greater changes brought about by commerce, industry, the fortunes of war, and the demands and desires of a restless society—first, the Dutch settlers, then the English, and later, the other groups of immigrants whose strengths and needs would change New York.

In the 1700s, the town of New York was located at the lower tip of Manhattan and reached northward only as far as Maiden Lane. Dominant commercially, the East River was the center of life. To the north was Greenwich village, a country retreat for the wealthy and a refuge in times of epidemic, and Harlem, nearly a day's journey away, was a distant settlement of farmers. The Bowery was a country road lined with old Dutch farmhouses, and Canal Street was still a canal.

For the first years of the eighteenth century, New York was in many ways like a small European seaport, preserving most of the same values with perhaps a bit more rowdy behavior at the waterfront. Its evolution was hastened, however, by the War for Independence. Long before a shot was fired, most people had chosen sides and the war was electric with domestic intrigues and foreign affairs. When it did come, the war was very hard on New York; after a brief period when General Washington was in control, the city became headquarters for the British. Private property was commandeered to billet soldiers, and in the years that followed, fighting and other destructive forces of war devastated the city. During the five harsh years of British occupation, New York was left in ruins and much of the populace fled. But after the war, people returned, and they rebuilt the city with remarkable dedication and speed. It was an extraordinary recovery,

2

topped only by New York's selection as the new nation's first capital, from 1790 to 1800. New York's preeminence was now firmly established, and its population nearly doubled between 1786 and 1796; commercially, politically, and socially, it was an exciting and important city. Yet even then, the city limits extended only one mile northward—to the area that became City Hall.

New York had been changing for hundreds of years—from wilderness to village, prosperous seaport, and nation's capital—but it was the nineteenth century that began the explosion of growth and change which we have come to regard as the quintessence of New York. Business prospered during the first decades of the century, and the opening of the Erie Canal in 1825 assured New York's position as center of commerce in the United States; the West was now open to the world through the port of New York. More than five hundred new businesses were started during this period, swelling the population and creating an immediate need for more construction.

Irish, Italian, and East European immigrants poured into New York, not exactly welcomed but grudgingly accepted as labor for the new industrial economy. They needed places to live, and the new businesses needed to be housed, as well. Building and more building ensued, and soon these properties were crowding the boundaries of fashionable residential areas. Predictably, the Dutch and Anglo-Saxon "old families" of means moved on to escape the proximity of commerce and its workers, and built fine new houses which were soon to be abandoned—crowded out once more by burgeoning industry—for newer and more elaborate mansions. Day by day, it seemed, New York continued to move uptown. And diarist Philip Hone complained, "New York is rebuilt once in ten years." (Doesn't that sound familiar?)

All at once the city's boundaries were expanding, the economy was booming, and the fabric of society had changed entirely. Threadbare at one extreme, at the other it was conspicuously opulent. The merchant class prospered, and enormous fortunes were made. Thrift was replaced by copious spending as an individual and municipal virtue.

There is no doubt that this great wealth made possible many improvements to the city. In 1842, the opening of the Croton Aqueduct provided access to "pure and wholesome" water for the first time. New York had entered a new era which included indoor plumbing, bathrooms, and a proper sewer system. Also around this time appeared the luxuries of central heating and gas lights. And by the end of the 1850s, work had begun on Central Park, a wonderful playground where the rich raced horses, skated, and went riding in their elegant carriages.

Entertainment, education, culture, and spiritual and social improvement were all highly esteemed and supported, to a great extent, by the city's new wealth. In 1853, New York had 272 churches. There were 13 parks and squares, 25 hotels on Broadway alone, theaters, minstrel halls, Barnum's American Museum, Franconi's Hippodrome, the Latting Observatory, and the dazzling Crystal Palace. Art institutions were established, and educational and benevolent organizations proliferated. The city held impressive receptions and celebrations, spending vast sums of money to fulfill civic pride. On the individual level, conspicuous consumption flourished, with parvenu and old money alike striving to outdo the other hosting dinners, parties, and balls, each more lavish than the one before.

Although the upper classes mightily enjoyed this climate of largesse, great amounts of money—particularly in the possession of newly rich upstarts—gave a new complexity to high society. At the beginning of the century and earlier, the social order was easily maintained: The old families, descendants of the original settlers, preserved their aristocracy through intermarriage. And if, over the years, some of these families did not remain wealthy—no matter. Their name assured them a place at the top.

New money complicated this simplicity. An enormous fortune was compelling in many ways, but it could not quite grant legitimacy. That final grace was achieved through a kind of merger which became acceptable during the so-called golden age of society in New York—the marriage of new money to old family name. One classic example of such a union was the marriage of Caroline Webster Schermerhorn to William Backhouse Astor, grandson of John Jacob Astor. Fifty million dollars were not sufficient to take the Astors into the upper reaches of society without the Schermerhorn alliance. Yet after the wedding, there were no limits; Caroline (Gene's first cousin) became the definitive leader during society's heyday and was known simply as *the* Mrs. Astor.

4

The Schermerhorns certainly qualified as old family. Jacob Janse Schermerhorn was in one of the first groups of Dutch settlers to arrive in the New Netherlands, as New York State was then called. Settling in Albany in 1626, he prospered during his lifetime there, in real estate and fur trading. His son, Symon, distinguished himself as a hero during the 1690 Indian Massacre at Schenectady and resettled in New York the following year. Soon afterwards, he purchased a large trading sloop and started a shipping business which was successful for generations. In the following century, during the War for Independence, the Schermerhorn family used their ships—a fleet grown from Symon's initial venture—to aid the patriots' cause for nationhood.

When the war was over, Peter Schermerhorn (Symon's son) played an important role in the city's development. An account of New York leaders in *The Old Merchants of New York* (1866) refers to Peter as "one of the founders of New York's rapid rise to eminence [who also] . . . was in many other ways a valuable citizen. He died . . . leaving a large property (for that age)."

It was during Peter's years as patriarch of the family that the Schermerhorns became especially active in acquiring New York city properties. Given his financial acumen (he was also a director of the Bank of New York), it is not surprising that the family had extensive real estate holdings in Manhattan and early investments in Brooklyn. Several place-names endure today to remind us of the family's former prominence: Schermerhorn Street in Brooklyn, Schermerhorn Hall at Columbia University, and at the South Street Seaport, Schermerhorn Row—a group of houses that Peter built on Fulton Street in the early 1800s.

Peter's son, John Schermerhorn, married Rebecca Stevens, daughter of Ebenezer Stevens who participated in the Boston Tea Party and was subsequently a Revolutionary War hero. Their son, George Stevens Schermerhorn, married Maria Isabella Grim, and had four children: George Stevens, Jr., Charles Augustus, Edward Eugene, and a daughter, Julia. Nothing is known about Julia's life. George became a lawyer, and along with his brother Charles, was active in several exclusive genealogical societies. (George was the father of Phil—to whom these letters were addressed.) Charles was a realtor and insurance broker who, according to his *New York Times* obituary in 1914, managed "the large family holdings." He was presi-

5

dent of the elite St. Nicholas Society and vestryman at Trinity Church. Following the tradition of military service passed down on both sides of the family, the sons served in the prestigious Seventh Regiment where their father in his youth had been Paymaster, a position of honor. And Gene and Charles served in the Civil War, though they each could have paid $300 for a substitute. Though they took civic responsibility quite seriously, this branch of the Schermerhorn family was apparently less inclined to be noticed in high society than various aunts, uncles, and cousins (including, of course, Mrs. William C. Schermerhorn, renowned social leader at the time, and *the* Mrs. Astor), and none of their names appears in lists of the social events of the day.

Reading these letters, we are inevitably made most curious about Gene—what he did in life, what kind of person he was. Ironically, he is the brother about whom the least is known. Unlike George and Charles, he seems to have had no ambition for prominence, and he was not a member of any of the elite organizations. Gene is listed intermittently in city directories with his home address, but never with a business address. He lived with his parents, and according to the family genealogy, he never married. We know that, as a youngster, Gene attended the Mechanics Society School where he could have learned a trade and studied a variety of subjects, including art, architecture, and science. From these letters we know that Gene was an enthusiastic amateur artist, but it seems unlikely that he ever studied art seriously or followed it as a profession. He is not listed in any of the professional directories of the day, and it is entirely possible that he just stayed home, enjoyed a leisurely life, and followed his interests without any pressing professional responsibilities—not uncommon then for a man of his class.

Of his earliest years, we know that Gene lived in Williamsburgh, Brooklyn. This small, prosperous village of merchants boomed in the 1830s because of good building sites and transportation to the center of the city in lower Manhattan. But when the dramatically growing economy and the beginning of immigration brought an influx of newcomers to the area, its character changed—and the value of its real estate dropped. And so, in 1845, George Schermerhorn moved his family out of Williamsburgh.

6

Unlike other Schermerhorns who lived in splendor in lower Manhattan, George and his family moved to West 23rd Street, out of the mainstream of "good" society. Whether this was due to limited money or a preference for peace and quiet, away from the city center, is not known. It *is* certain, however, that in 1845, living on 23rd Street was living in the country, and that the Schermerhorn family's moving there was in the vanguard of the city's northward push.

New York's development proceeded (with a few notable variations) according to the Grid Plan—a layout of streets up to 155th Street devised by the city fathers in 1807. The plan was remarkable in its attempt to look ahead and provide for the city's future greatness, though it did not anticipate the explosive growth that New York was to experience almost immediately. Much of the plan remains in effect today, incorporating corrections to certain flaws that were realized before long. It became clear, for example, that more good roads out of town were needed and that the continuation of Broadway was more important to the city's future than the parade ground at 23rd Street where Broadway stopped. The Schermerhorns' move to 23rd Street just one step ahead of the city set a family precedent that would prevail for years to come; after 23rd Street, they moved to West 26th Street, West 53rd Street, and finally, Gene moved to the Boulevard (as Broadway above 59th Street was called) sometime before he wrote the ninth of the letters to Phil.

Perhaps it was this propensity to stay slightly ahead of the growing city that prompted Gene to look back over the ground he had covered and record it for Phil. Perhaps his father's death in 1885, the year before, and his mother's advanced age compelled him to go back and recapture a bygone time and place. We can do no more than speculate on the precise motivation behind these writings, but we can appreciate, with a dimension beyond his own, his desire to pass along eye-witness knowledge of what it was like in simple, rustic New York—before electricity, the telephone, and the continuing impact of immigration and commerce. In 1886, Fifth Avenue was an important thoroughfare, completely built up; Gene remembered when it was a muddy rutted road, sparsely settled. Once fashionable and elegant, the lower east side was now filled with tenements, and 23rd Street, his first home in Manhattan, had gone from an area of small

7

farms to a wealthy residential neighborhood to a busy commercial center, bordered on the west by a red-light district.

Many more changes have taken place in New York and in the rest of the world since the 1880s, and we, today's readers of Gene Schermerhorn's letters, can only marvel at the contrast among the three periods—the 1840s-1850s as described by Gene, the 1880s when he wrote, and our own time, the 1980s—a triple perspective. And we can certainly understand his wonder at the enormous changes that took place over a thirty-odd year period, for we, today, constantly find ourselves surprised by the disappearance of old buildings which are shortly thereafter replaced by bigger and better—or, at least, newer ones. At this very moment, we are witnessing the same dramatic shifts in neighborhoods that Gene did—once-solid residential neighborhoods that drop out of favor while other shabby or commercial districts become "gentrified" and chic. Today, however, we are more apt to try to preserve some of our architectural and historical past than people of Gene's day. While Gene is often nostalgic about elements of his childhood which had disappeared forever, he never suggests that all these changes are anything but necessary and inevitable. Our recently acquired ability to question tearing down the old makes Gene's letters even more significant to us—almost like stopping the wrecker's ball in mid-air.

It is, in fact, like finding a cache of historical treasure to read Gene's account of his early activities and interests, many of which are quite outside our knowledge and experience. Putting them together with the other available personal accounts of the time, we have history that lives, a fascinating and human picture of mid-nineteenth century life. Gene shows us a wonderfully free and adventurous boyhood in the wilds above 20th Street, roaming at will through farmlands and woods, playing by the rivers and ponds, exploring train yards, factories, and uncharted territory, running after and eventually joining the volunteer fire fighters.

The Volunteer Fire Department (one of the great passions of Gene's early life) was the only means the city had to fight fires. Gene was a member as quite a young boy, and in his letters to Phil, he describes with enthusiasm the fire fighting procedures as well as the excitement, rituals, and camaraderie. Other accounts than his assert that there was indeed a special character and spirit to the volunteer fire companies which were not matched by the paid fire department that became part of the municipal system in 1865. Department observers reported that the old volunteer firemen had managed to reach the fires more quickly than their salaried counterparts. And although the volunteers received no pay, pride in their engines and companies—and rivalry with other companies—was so strong that they contributed to the upkeep and elaborate decoration of the engines. Immortalized in the splendid prints by Currier and Ives, the fire fighters were deeply appreciated and honored by the public at large, not the least of which included the Swedish Nightingale, Jenny Lind, who donated $3,000 of the proceeds from her Castle Garden concert to their fund.

Beyond the need to put out fires, the volunteer fire company served as a social and political center of New York life. Politics, once the bailiwick of gentlemen, had been left to the feisty newcomers, mainly the Irish, and a would-be politician could make or break his career after fire fighting hours. Mayors were elected on the strength of their importance in fire companies; the infamous Boss Tweed, for one, began his career in his local volunteer fire department. Despite the fact that these fire companies existed within a highly class-conscious society, the volunteers were from all classes and mingled freely while battling fires, of course, but at the celebrated torchlight parades and annual Firemen's Balls, too. According to one account of the day, "A better organized body of men does not exist . . . embracing all or most of the young and active citizens of every class and rank of society."

Gene recalled all this and more to share with his nephew, Phil, and we are the beneficiaries. It is a fascinating world that he describes, with detail after detail making history come alive for us, so many years later. But every bit as wonderful as the story he tells is the way that he tells it. Gene Schermerhorn wrote with gentle affection for the time that had gone past, with interest and appreciation for the present in which he was living, and with wonder as he looked toward the future, guessing that Phil might see changes far beyond his imagination.

Gene himself lived until 1922, witnessing along the way so many innovations that we take for granted: the introduction of electricity,

9

the telephone, telegraph, mass transportation, the automobile, and radio. He saw the Statue of Liberty installed on Bedloe's (later, Liberty) Island, the consolidation of Manhattan and the surrounding boroughs into New York City, the building of the Brooklyn Bridge and Grand Central Station (not once but twice), and he saw the Great World War.

Gene was right. The growth of the city in the nineteenth century was staggering, and continued so into the twentieth. Phil lived till 1952, more than a hundred years from his uncle's loving reminiscences, fulfilling his Uncle Gene's prophecy of seeing undreamed of changes in New York. As we approach the new century, not even twenty years away, we are brought full circle to that prophecy and wonder, as Gene did with Phil, about the transformations that today's ten-year-olds may see in their lifetime.

Phil left no child to inherit the homemade history that had been given him, and the letters were lost for many years. At one time discarded and found in a thrift shop, they passed from hand to hand before they were discovered by the publisher of this book. Their rediscovery is a happy event, for any time we can reclaim a lost portion of our history, we are the richer and perhaps wiser for it. *Letters to Phil* is published now for everyone who has ever wondered, remembered, and dreamed—and for those who are not old enough to do that yet; and thus, Gene's gift to Phil is a gift to us all.

Editorial Notes

The letters appear in this book almost exactly as Gene Schermerhorn wrote them. The only differences are the correction of two misspelled proper names and a few small punctuation changes considered necessary to clarify meaning for the modern reader. As few changes as possible were made, for it was felt that Gene's syntax and punctuation are an intrinsic part of his story.

Throughout the letters, various words or phrases are marked with an asterisk, indicating their inclusion in the Historical Glossary at the back of the book. The glossary is divided into ten sections, corresponding to the letters, and the words are listed in each section according to the order in which they appear in the letter. At the end of the glossary is an index of all these terms, giving the number of the letter where it first appears as well as its glossary page.

125 West 53rd Street
December 8th, 1886

My Dear Phil,

I propose to write for you some things which I can remember about New York when I was a boy; for I think that some day—when you are a little older perhaps, you will like to know something about it. I doubt if you care much for such things now, but I will try both to amuse you at present with what I and other boys did and to interest you when you are older and can appreciate the great changes that have taken place. It is not so very long ago and I don't mean to tell you any "old mans yarns" for I am not quite a grandfather but only

Your Uncle Gene

No. 1

It seems hard to believe that Twenty-third Street—which is the first street in the city of which I remember anything, could have changed so much in so short a time. The rural scenes, the open spaces, have vanished; and the small and quiet residences, many of them built entirely of wood, have given place to huge piles of brick and stone, and to iron and plate-glass fronts of the stores which now line the street.

I was six years old when we moved to New York from Williamsburgh* in 1848. We went to live in a house in this street just west of Sixth Avenue. It was far out of town then, for people lived about 8th Street, on lower Fifth Avenue,* and the cross streets about Washington Square; and even that was considered quite up town, for a great many very nice people lived in Lafayette Place and even in East Broadway and around St. Johns Square.*

This will give you an idea of the house; right next door was a small farm or truck-garden extending nearly to Seventh Avenue. Across the way were the stables of the 6th Ave Omnibus line; the stages starting here and going down Sixth Avenue, 8th Street and Broadway to the Battery. They

afterwards started from Forty-sixth Street. I shall
have more to tell about these Stage Lines for at this
time there were no horse cars. Twenty-third Street
and in fact all the streets in the neighborhood were
unpaved. Here was my playground and a good one
it was. There certainly was plenty of room, plenty
of dirt (clean dirt) and plenty of boys; what more
could be desired! Of course I was too young at first
to enjoy it all as I afterwards did, and your father
and Uncle Charlie had most of the fun.

Kite flying, "How Many Miles," marbles and
something we called Base Ball were the great
games.* Think of flying kites now with all the
telegraph poles and wires not to speak of the
"Cops." Marbles was played in a great ring four or
five feet across marked out on the smooth hard
dirt; not in the miserable way they do now—a
little spot of bare earth about two feet by four and

three or four glass marbles, as I saw some boys playing the other day. A handfull or two of marbles were put in the ring; and then you would hear shouts of "knuckle down," "fen dubs," "fen everything," etc. etc. The good shots would have bags half as large as their heads, full of "migs," "China Alleys" and "Real agates." And then a crowd of "Loafers" from some other street would make their appearance, and everyone would grab the marbles and run, or else stand and fight and then there *would* be a time.

But as I say, I was too young to do much more than look on in admiration of my elder brothers. Yet I had some fun too: one of my amusements was to chase the pigs* that ran in Sixth Avenue and try (in vain) to catch them with a lassoo made in good shape from old clothes line. Now I suppose a boy would buy a revolver and go west to shoot Indians.

ℕo. 2

December 19th, 1886

I have told you about the little farm next door to our house: both sides of the street all the way over to Ninth Avenue were much the same in appearance. There were very few houses and only at or about the corners of the Avenues. The rest was all open lots and market-truck gardens; beyond the Ninth Avenue, on the south side of the street and extending across Tenth Avenue—or to the river front, for 11th and 12th Avenues have been added since, was the Clement C. Moore place; the house was built before the Revolution and the place was known as Chelsea.* Some of our soldiers were

quartered here during that war and General Washington is known to have visited it. A British ship, sailing up the river one day, fired a shot which lodged in one of the partitions. The grounds, when I remember them first, covered the entire block and were surrounded by a high stone wall. They were elevated above the street and were beautifully laid out with trees and shrubberies. I have often played over these grounds.

Across the way, was built somewhere about this time London Terrace, a fine row of houses set back from the street and extending the length of the block; many of them still retain their original appearance. In the rear on Twenty-fourth Street was another row, smaller and less pretentious, called Chelsea Terrace.

One day about this time, I remember that I started out with a friend somewhat older than myself—probably one of the "pig hunters"—for a walk. We wandered over to Fourth Avenue* and followed the railroad up to see the engines, which were attached to the cars at 32nd Street: the cars being drawn by horses through the streets from down town. The Passenger station was at 26th Street and the Freight depot at Centre and White Streets. There was no Fourth Avenue above this but we wandered on over the rocks where Park Avenue is until we had got as far as 42nd Street. Of course I had no idea of where I was and felt tired and hungry, so when at last a bee stung me, I wanted to go home. We got on an empty car going down to steal a ride and when we reached 32nd

Street I thought it time to get off and so jumped and naturally landed on my head. An old woman picked me up and carried me into a little rum shop,* where someone bathed my head and finally they started me off for home. What became of my friend I don't know. Some time about Five O'Clock I managed to get into Twenty-third Street, where my Uncle found me and brought me home. I think this was but the beginning for I have ever since been fond of exploring the streets, and as a boy I knew more of the city than most boys do.

When I was seven years old there occurred the Astor Place Riot* where the Seventh Regiment fired on the mob, and I remember being taken down there a few days afterwards and seeing the marks made by the bullets on the houses and the broken windows of the Opera House.* Your Grandfather's uncle Horatio Gates Stevens lived at Broadway and 8th Street then, and at his house I always made a New Year's* call. I usually received a Two-Dollar-and-a-half gold piece on such occasions.

No. 3

December 26th, 1886

At the corner of Twenty-third Street and Fifth Avenue was the country seat of the Mildenburgher family: a beautiful rural picture with gardens and orchards extending along the street. I remember very well the apple trees drooping over the sidewalks, which were often covered with fallen blossoms. On the north side of the street were the grounds of a then, and for many years before this, famous road house known as Corporal Thompson's. This house faced Madison Square near where the main entrance of the Fifth Avenue

Madison Cottage~ Corporal Thompson Propr.
N.B. Stages start every 4 minutes

Hotel now is. On the grounds in the rear were held the "cattle fairs" where prize cattle and fine horses were to be seen—the Horse Show of those days. I remember a convenient hole in the fence on the 24th Street side through which *some* boys entered "D.H." On the 23rd Street side was a building at first a barn but then occupied by Engine Co. No. 25, which company I afterward became better acquainted with. These grounds were afterwards used by Franconi's Hippodrome *—a sort of Madison Square Garden place which we thought very wonderful.

From here, going west to 6th Avenue on each side of the street were rows of small wooden houses; very pretty they were with their vine covered porches and balconies. At 6th Avenue were some three-story brick stores and dwellings. Sixth Avenue was open as far as 43rd St. where it ended abruptly in more market gardens; the street being filled up far above the rows of vegetables growing there. All above this was country indeed with but few houses except on the principal avenues and on some of the cross streets which were open.

This was in the neighborhood of 5th Avenue and 45th St. and will give an idea of most of the city above 23rd Street at this time. Far away were Bloomingdale and Yorkville, Manhattanville and Harlem.

I was Foreman of an Engine Company now. The members were uniformed in red shirts and we raced up and down the street and made lots of noise, but we never got very far away from home for fear of being attacked by some rival company. A fight was a serious matter, from a small beginning sometimes ending in a big row with 20 or 30 boys on a side, and the stones flew thick through the air.

Our engine looked something like this, and when the water was turned on and the brakes were worked it really looked very well.

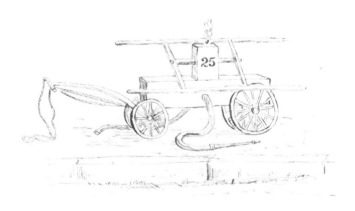

George Christy—the first of Negro Minstrels, lived opposite our house and of course we boys were full of their performances. We blacked our faces and sang negro minstrel songs in our front basement. George Christy* brought out a piece which he called "Schermerhorn's Boy" which some ill-natured people said was meant for me.

No. 4

January 9th, 1887

Broadway, at this time (1854) from Twenty-third Street down to Union Square was well built up with small houses and shops—mostly frame buildings, two or three stories high. There were some fine houses at Union Square and a Hotel at Fourteenth Street called the "Spingler House." Next to this was Dr. Cheever's church; this was a handsome building, and when it was pulled down to make room for Tiffany's store, part of it was rebuilt in 53rd St., part in East 14th St. and part in 36th St. The Park itself was an oval in shape and was surrounded by an iron railing about ten feet high with fine granite gate-posts. The lower part of Fifth Avenue was occupied by houses then thought very fine. At the corner of 18th Street were two handsome marble houses built in the Italian style: they stood back from the street and had gardens. The most fashionable part of the Avenue was below 14th Street, and here the people used to walk after church.

  We went to the Church of the Holy Communion* at 6th Ave. and 20th Street, further up town than any church I remember at this time except St. James, the Hamilton Square, and the Bloomingdale Church. Your Father, Uncles and

Aunt went to the Church Schools founded by Dr. Muhlenberg, and I could tell you a great deal about our doings there and how we dressed the church at Christmas.

St. James Church

When my Uncle Augustus died in 1855 the funeral went on foot from our house to the church. The coffin was covered with a long black pall and was borne on the shoulders of men. Such a sight would be a strange one in our streets now I think.

Up town at this time was almost inaccessible. Of course there was no Central Park. Third Avenue was open to Harlem passing through Yorkville which was quite a large village about 86th Street "midway between Harlem and the City." The Harlem R.R. here passed through an open cut in the rocks, there were a good many houses strung along Third Avenue but mostly in clusters like that at "Rose Hill" near 35th Street.

These houses were on Lexington Ave near 37th Street. All around in this neighborhood which was Murray Hill, * there were others of like character and appearance. There was one at the corner of Fifth Avenue and 37th Street which remained until within a very few years: on the opposite corner where the "Brick Church" now stands, was a beautiful house built in castellated style and standing on a high terrace. This was the Waddell place. Fifth Ave. was open beyond this: at the corner of 40th Street was the "Croton Cottage."

From here on, it was in a very rough condition being partly graded to 59th Street. At 45th Street on the East side was "Bulls's Head," a cattle yard covering an entire block. Opposite was the Colored Orphan Asylum* which was burned during the riots of '63. Near 59th Street were some rocks towering above the street where at a later day

we boys delighted to climb up and touch the telegraph wires. Beyond this was the "Arsenal," then
used by the State and kept full of muskets, etc. and
the "Powder house" where the ammunition was
stored.

Eighth Avenue was open to Harlem, and in
connection with Harlem Lane (now St. Nicholas
Ave.) was the great road for fast driving. Broadway—known as Bloomingdale Road from 23rd
Street up to Carmansville (152nd Street)—passed
through Bloomingdale and Manhattanville; from
Carmansville to Kingsbridge it was called the
Kingsbridge Road. It was throughout its entire
length another famous road for driving.

There was a line of stages on 3rd Avenue to
Harlem, and one on Bloomingdale Road to Manhattanville; these, with the Harlem and Hudson

River Railroads were the only means of getting up town. In 1853 the "Crystal Palace"* was built and the World's Fair was held in it. This was where Bryant Park now is. Houses and shops began to spring up around it, and the Sixth Avenue horse cars commenced running to 42nd Street soon after; also the 3rd and 8th Avenue cars to about 59th Street. There were lines of stages down town on many streets and avenues but still hardly anything of the kind above 42nd Street. About this time they were building Trinity Chapel and we could still walk there "across lots" from our house.

Bloomingdale Church

No. 5

January 23rd, 1887

It seems to me that we had a great deal more snow*
then, than we have now: there used to be good
sleighing in Broadway for weeks at a time, and all
the stage lines ran huge open sleighs,* in place of
the usual stages. These same sleighs were the
means of our having some of the jolliest times we
ever had. In the evenings, large parties would get
on the sleighs and ride down to the South ferry and
back and oh! what fun: such shouting and snow
balling and such a good time generally.

The sleighs all had at least four horses and
sometimes six, eight, or ten. I have known sixteen
and twenty on some of the larger ones. People used
to crowd in and hang on the outside, while there

33

always seemed room for one more. Someone would shout "Come right up here by the stove." Of couse there was no stove but they would crowd up all the same. On the box were sometimes men dressed in fancy costumes or like old women. I remember once seeing some men with huge tin trumpets eight or ten feet long. Every small boy who could not ride, seemed to feel like taking it out of those who could by pelting them with snowballs; but no one seemed to mind it much.

Down on the Battery was Castle Garden; this was once a round stone fort like the one on Governors Island but had been given up as a fort and was used for a concert hall and for exhibitions and such purposes: the Fair of the American Institute was held here. It stood out in the water and was approached over a bridge. The Battery has since

been filled out. The building was burned and after a while was rebuilt in its present shape.

There were none of those magnificent office buildings now so common in the lower part of the city. A building of any kind six stories high was very rare. I can recall but two or three such in the entire city. Where the Mutual Life Building now stands was the Post-Office. This was a historic building and was formerly known as the Middle Dutch Church: it was used as a stable by the British Troops during the Revolution.

No. 1 Broadway was another noted building. It was built in 1742 and was occupied during that war by the different British Commanders. It was a very large and handsome house and must have seemed palatial in those days. It occupied the site of the present Washington Building and at the time it was demolished (only two or three years ago) was one of the oldest buildings in the City.

There were other fine churches down town besides St. Paul's and Trinity: among them were the North Dutch Church at the corner of Fulton and William Sts.; the Brick Church in Park Row where the "Times" office now is; and which is now at the corner of 5th Ave and 34th St., and St. George's in Beekman St. At the latter your Great grandfather had a pew and in the churchyard his father was buried (Peter Schermerhorn).

The City Hall Park was surrounded by a tall iron fence, and at the south end where the Post Office stands was a fine fountain and some large trees. Opposite St. Paul's Church was Barnum's

St. George's

Museum, a wonderful place containing a theatre and four floors packed with all sorts of strange things. It was a delight to go there on Saturday afternoons. This place was burned in 1865.

The other theatres were all down town of course. Burton's in Chamber St., The National in Chatham St., The Broadway near Worth St., and Wallachs near Broome St. The New York Hospital was on the west side of Broadway opposite Pearl St. and had extensive grounds with grass and trees.

This very unattractive looking place was exactly where the entrance to the Brooklyn bridge now is. The houses were occupied chiefly by second-hand clothing dealers and mock auction rooms,* and the poor countryman or sailor had a hard time of it when he found himself in the neighborhood.

Along the river front the wharfs were crowded with full-rigged ships and barks, and of course the difference in rig from that of the steamer of to-day and the greater number of vessels (for one steamer is equal to many ships) made a perfect "forest of masts." The bowsprits of some of these large ships—famous clippers they were, noted for their quick voyages—in many cases projected far across the street and seemed to knock at the windows of the stores along South Street. Farther up on this street were the Dry Docks and ship yards where all was bustle and activity; several ships being on the stocks at the same time. America led the world then in ship-building.

No. 6

February 6th, 1887

From 1854 to 1857 I went to the "Mechanics Society School"* in Crosby St. near Broome, and used to walk there and back every day. In the afternoons I often walked home with some of the other boys and in this way became familiar with almost every part of the city above Broome Street.

St. Thomas' Church was at the corner of Broadway and Houston Street; opposite to it was a row of small two-storied wooden houses; many of them low grog shops—a very bad neighborhood.

Tiffany's store was near Prince Street and next to it was a church. All about here was the great shopping centre, although many large stores—among them A.T. Stewarts dry goods store at Chambers St.—were much lower down.

These houses were in Broadway facing Waverly Place: they were of white marble and were built about the same time as the famous "Colonnade Row" nearly in the rear on Lafayette Place. This was at that time (somewhere in the forties) the "swell" part of the town.

One day a fire broke out in the "City Assembly Rooms" near the school and some of the boys managed to get out at noon; that was the last of us for that day. The fire was a very large one, five buildings were burned in Broadway, and three in Crosby Street. It was dreadfully cold, and the water froze in the hose: everything was covered with ice and immense icicles hung from the buildings. It was a wonderful sight. This is the first large fire that I remember seeing.

In 1855 we moved to this house—No. 52 West 26th St. All around were vacant lots and only about a dozen houses on the block—mostly new. On the corner opposite was a large Carriage Manufactory which I had the run of and of course enjoyed very much. At the corner of Broadway

where the St. James Hotel is, was a lumber yard with two or three big trees: it was a good playground and we built houses of the lumber: we even dragged the boards up into the trees and built houses there much to the disgust of the workmen; but we did not mind for they could never catch us in such a place.

We used to skate on two ponds which were on the line of 32nd and 33rd Sts., one near Broadway and the other at about Madison Avenue—right back of the "round house" of the Harlem R.R. We were skating here one day on what we called "pompey ice," when your Uncle Charlie fell in and cut his hand badly. He showed the scar the other day when I asked if he remembered the pond. These ponds were on the line of an old brook which had its rise near 42nd St. and Broadway and running around the southerly side of Murray Hill finally found its way to the East River at Kip's Bay (35th Street).

Park Avenue from 34th St to 42nd St where the tunnel is, was a rock cut through which the Harlem R.R. tracks ran. This was a favorite place for Uncle Charlie and myself to spend our Saturdays playing among the rocks and watching the trains. On other Saturdays, we would take long walks up town, sometimes to the shot tower* at 51st Street and East River. Near this was the "Beekman Mansion."

This house was built in 1764 and during the Revolution was a favorite residence of the British

General Howe. A mantelpiece from one of the rooms is now in the N.Y. Historical Society and is a fine example of the "Colonial style," the fireplace is of old blue and white Dutch tiles.

Sometimes we would walk in the region which is now the Central Park. It was a very rough and rocky place, with plenty of woods and scattered trees and very few houses except "Squatters" shanties. Not many streets were opened through it but they were marked out with small marble "monuments" as they were called.

Opposite the Crystal Palace on 42nd St was the "Latting Observatory."* This was a tower built of wood and two hundred and eighty feet high. From the top a splendid view could be had. It was burned one night in the year 1856 and the light it made was so great that we could see to read by it in our house in 26th Street.

No. 7

February 20th, 1887

It is now time for me to tell you about something that was beginning to be of the greatest interest to me. I mean the Fires, and the Firemen, and "running with the masheen." I believe that the boys of New York have always been crazy on this subject, if I may judge from what I have heard, of the times when my uncles were boys. My uncle Phil was living with us, and he had been a Fireman when he was a young man. The Fire Department* was a volunteer one: that is, the men served without pay. Some of the companies were composed of most respectable men; the majority were mechanics and some were of a pretty rough class. The engine I have drawn for you was the one nearest to our house, and of course the one with which all the

boys in the neighborhood "ran." "She lay" on Broadway, between 26th and 27th Streets. On the opposite side of Broadway was a famous tree—the last of its race, an immense buttonball or sycamore: one of the ornaments of the old Varian farm, which comprised all the land in this vicinity once—but this was some years before I can remember.

Often at a fire when the men were tired and were working slowly, someone would shout "Now one for the Big Tree" and then they would "shake

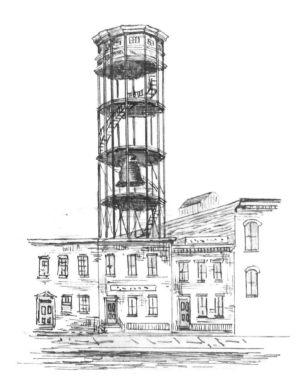

her up with a will." Every company had its allotted districts to which it proceeded when an alarm was given. This was done by men who occupied Bell towers in various parts of the city: sometimes built of iron, like the one in Macdougal Street; and sometimes of wood like this one. When these men saw a fire, they struck an alarm on immense bells which could be heard a long distance. I have often

heard the City Hall bell in our house in 26th
Street. We could recognize the different bells and
always listened and counted the strokes.

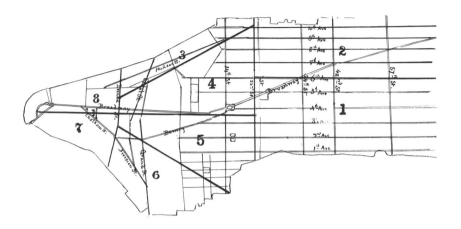

The districts were arranged like this. No. 25
ran to the Second and Fourth Districts and at one
time, to the Third also: so you see we sometimes
had a good long run. We often ran to the corner of
6th Ave and 52nd St when the bell "struck for the
2nd," the reason being, that there was a match
factory near the corner, just across the Avenue
from where you live, which was always catching
fire. When the fire was in some other district, we
ran with some friendly company, usually with
Pacific Engine No. 28, or Metamora Hose No. 29.
The latter company being considered quite a swell
company, as was also Zephyr Hose No. 61 with
which we sometimes ran. These companies all ran
to the 5th District.

When I was down town at a later day, I sometimes ran with Southwark Engine No. 38. This was a huge "double-decker," the largest and heaviest engine in the Department. She was so heavy that they used a drag rope when going down hill to keep her from running over the men.

I have spoken of friendly companies. There were others that were not friends and were continually fighting. Dreadful battles were common, growing out of races and general rivalry. Sometimes there would be two or three hundred men and boys pulling an engine, and a race at such a time was very exciting, even without a fight. Of course, the boys took up these affairs in their smaller way, and fought on every occasion. It was not safe for a boy who ran with 25 to be seen near 24th Street and 8th Ave., for instance, where Mazeppa Engine No. 48 lay, or near 58th Street and Broadway, the home of Black Joke Engine No. 33: the latter in particular, having the reputation of being great fighters.

When the bells began to strike for a fire it was a strange sight: every man or boy interested, would

stop short in whatever he was doing and listen, if he heard his district—and one round of the bells was enough, the streets were instantly alive with running men and boys. The first to arrive at the engine house would dash in, and seizing the tongue would yell "Fire in the 4th," or "Jefferson Market's hitting two." To be at the "tongue" was a post of honor and the Fireman, or sometimes the runner who had it was entitled to hold the "pipe" at the fire—a post of danger as well as honor. The engine was immediately run out and sometimes with just men enough to move her, but gradually numbers were added and the call was constantly for more rope until there was a crowd and we seemed to fairly fly.

Arriving at the fire, a hydrant was sought, and the hose was attached and led to the fire: the brakes were then let down, and soon the Fireman's voice would be heard from the burning building, shouting, "Start your water, Twenty-five." Then with a yell the men would begin to "break her down" and this would go on with relays of willing arms at the breaks until the fire was out, when the Foreman would call "'Vast Twenty-Five" and then a few minutes later "Take up" and "Man your ropes" and we would return home.

Oh! It was vastly exciting and had a wonderful attraction for me. Day or night I was always listening for the fire bells. They would always wake me from the soundest sleep. My clothes were all laid in readiness to be occupied with as little delay as possible, and I could get out of the house in less time than you could imagine. But of course this was not till I was old enough to be out at night. Now I have written a long letter but have not told all I had to tell by any means. I have not said anything about some fires that I can remember or about the great Torchlight Parades but must leave all that for another letter.

This is the typical Fire Laddie of the East Side, Mose the Bowery Boy.*

No. 8

March 13th, 1887

This is a view at Fifth Avenue and 59th Street looking down the Avenue. It will give you an idea of how it looked in 1857. The large buildings are the R.C. Orphan Asylum, St. Luke's Hospital, and in the distance, the Crystal Palace. The latter was burned in 1858, and being all iron and glass, and filled with the Exhibition of the American Institute, it made a most beautiful fire.

On Sixth Avenue from 57th St. to 59th and beyond, was a famous skating pond, surrounded by high rocks far above the level of the present streets. This pond was on a branch of a large brook, which started at about Sixth Avenue and

Sixth Avenue at 56th Street

46th St; it followed the line of the Avenue to this pond and then turned off to the east, joining the main brook which had its rise among the woods and rocks of Central Park. Crossing 5th Avenue near 57th St. the brook widened out into a large pond which extended over to near 3rd Avenue, being crossed by the embankment of the Harlem R.R. and one or two streets. I remember how disgusted we boys felt when Madison Avenue was filled in, for it cut up and spoiled our pond. We knew this as Beekman's Pond: our fathers called it Sunfish Pond*; on a part of it on the east of Fourth Ave. at about 61st Street I once fell through the ice with two other boys, and we all came very near being drowned. The brook flowed on through low and wet ground and finally emptied into the East River at Turtle Bay (46th Street).

One of our favorite Saturday walks was up the Bloomingdale* Road. At 50th Street we passed this house: an old Dutch farm house, but I don't know its history. Beyond this, the houses became

54

more and more scattered and one could get glimps-
es of the river and the Jersey shore, here and there.

At 77th Street we came to Fernando
Wood's* place: the house is still standing, but it
will soon be gone, as it is directly in the line of the
street. West End Avenue now runs just back of the
trees in the rear of the house, and beyond that, is
Riverside Park and Drive, which was then all wild
and unoccupied land.

No. 9

272 Boulevard
January 15th, 1888

When writing my last letter to you, I did not know that in a few months I would be living in the very locality that I was trying to describe to you as it looked in my younger days. Fernando Wood's house, which I have drawn for you is already gone, 77th Street having been opened and taking away the larger part of it. A short distance farther up the Bloomingdale Road stood this house. It was known as "Burnhaus" and was kept as a road-house or stopping place for people driving out on the Bloomingdale Road. The house is still standing but is sadly changed in appearance. There we often left the road on our walks and turned down a

foot-path, now 79th St. to the river where we spent the day among the rocks and trees.

Returning once more to the East Side, I remember on the line of the Harlem R.R. at what is now 49th Street was "Potters field": a place where paupers and all the unclaimed dead of the city were buried. This "Potters Field" was formerly at Washington Square, but at this time the latter place was a very pretty park and here the Fall Inspections of the Militia were held. The Regiments had no armories as they have now but each company had a place for themselves, where they kept their muskets and had their drills. The Company of the Seventh Regiment* to which your father belonged had a room on Broadway near Houston Street, as did also some other companies of the same Regiment. Very few of the Regiments were even uniformed alike.

The East side was somewhat more built up than the west but was still very much "out of town." On the Bowery at 6th Street was the "Hay Scale" where the loads of hay brought in on that side of the city were weighed. Facing this was the "Gotham Inn," quite a noted sporting tavern. On the corner of 3rd Avenue and 13th Street stood an old pear tree, which was planted on Gov. Stuyvesant's farm in 1647.

On the west side of 5th Avenue at 45th Street was the Colored Orphan Asylum burned during the Draft Riots* in 1863. Opposite this also on 5th Avenue was "Bull's Head" or the cattle yards. There were few houses above this until you came to Yorkville. Extending from 66th to 69th St. and from Third to Fifth Ave. was Hamilton Square. This was never used as a park but was given up for that purpose when the Central Park was laid out. Here stood St. James Church which I have already drawn for you and near by was laid with great ceremony the corner stone of what was to be the Washington Monument. I wonder what ever became of it.

Near 80th St. a lane commenced which led to the East River near 86th St. This was the entrance to a number of beautiful country seats scattered along the high bank of the river, owned by the Astors, Crugers, Schermerhorns, Jones, Princes, Gracies, Rhinelanders and Waddingtons and among them your Great Great Grandfather's.

This house was torn down last spring and the site is now covered with stores and flats.

No. 10

November 16th, 1888

From 63rd to 80th St. and from 3rd Ave. to the river was a beautiful piece of woodland with hills and dales, brooks and noble old trees. It belonged to the Jones' and Schermerhorns and was known as "Jones' Woods."* It was a favorite place for pic-nics and excursions.

"Hell Gate" Ferry at the Foot of 86th St.

Yorkville* was a small village with its centre about 3rd Avenue and 86th Street and spreading a few blocks each way. Above 92nd St. Harlem Commons began. This was the low land extending from the East River at 90th St. to the Hudson at 129th St. (Manhattanville). It was cut up into farms and intersected by creeks running in from both rivers. At 109th St. and 2nd Ave. was the "Red House," a road house with a race track and base-ball ground. Harlem* was like another village extending from 125th St. along the 2nd, 3rd and 4th Avenues to the Harlem River.

Harlem Bridge at the End of Third Avenue

Other bridges crossed the river at 4th Avenue (Railroad), 8th Ave (McComb's Dam) and King's Bridge on the line of the Bloomingdale Road. High Bridge could only be reached by a long drive or by boat.

Now my dear Phil I have tried to tell you what this great city was like when I was a boy but little older than yourself, and I hope I have succeeded in interesting you somewhat. I have begun with my earliest recollections of New York and I will leave it now about 1856 when the population was only

629,810—less than half what it was at the last census in 1880. It is estimated now at over 1,500,000.

I cannot help looking forward and wondering, if it can possibly be that you can tell of as great changes. It is my firm belief that you will be able to do so and that you will live to see the entire island as thickly built as it is now below 59th St. and perhaps the district above the Harlem also. Or it may be that you will see changes that I don't even dream of, although my faith in the future of New York is unbounded. I could go on and write many more letters, telling of things which I have hinted at and of interesting events of a later date. I have preferred to stop here in my story which perhaps has not been very interesting after all and yet I hope you will sometimes enjoy reading what has given me so much pleasure to write for you.

Your Loving Uncle Gene

Phil Schermerhorn,
An Afterword

119 West 74th St.
May 10th, 1890

Dear Ed,

This morning I went down to the "Boulevard."
They were putting down the tar and small stone.
They had a Steam Roller something like this!

    I rode my Bicycle up and down all the day and
I had a very good time. Yesterday I went to the
theatre. They had two plays in English and one in
French. I could understand some words they
said!!!!!!
    I hope you will *come down* to the City and
then *come up* in the "Country" that is, 74th St.
We all miss you very much. Even Sister said *SHE
MISSED YOU!!!* I went around to 272 Boulevard.
Grandma was well. Constance was there.
    Y I d E M i u s o s

it means Ed I miss you!!

Your Loving Brother Phil

Though Philip Grim Schermerhorn was only eight years old when his Uncle Gene began his series of ten letters, Gene must somehow have sensed that here was a family member whose disposition was akin to his own. The letters were surely well received by Phil for he emulates them in this illustrated letter to his brother, which the publisher found with Gene's letters to Phil.

Like his Uncle Gene, Phil grew up to be the quiet one in a rather public family. His brother, Edward Gibert, was active in the military throughout his life (the Seventh Regiment, a Schermerhorn tradition) and served as Military Secretary to the Governor of New York during the early 1900s. Phil did not appear at all in the 1911 City Directory, but in the 1920-21 edition, he is listed as living with his brother. Like Gene, Phil did not appear in the professional directories of his day. He married, but as far as we know, never had children.

The little information available concerning his adult life comes from his obituary in *The New York Times*. In 1952, Phil died suddenly of a heart attack at the age of seventy-four. He was one of the ninth generation of Schermerhorns in New York State. He had lived in New York City at 205 East 78th Street and was survived by his widow, Elsa Carla Fuelslein Schermerhorn.

The *Times* described him as "a painter of landscapes and portraits." Whether he was a professional or an amateur artist is not known; all his work is apparently lost.

Historical Glossary

Letter No. 1

ST. JOHN'S SQUARE. Bordered by Varick, Beach, Hudson, and Laight Streets, St. John's Square, or Park, was a prime residential area of New York in the early 1800s. Alexander Hamilton and General Schuyler were among the homeowners in this section, which was described in contemporary accounts as having a particularly European flavor. The park itself was notable on two accounts: First, because it was planted with a variety of unusual and choice trees, and second, because its use was reserved for keyholders—owners of surrounding houses. (St. John's and Gramercy were the only two private parks in the city.)

As the city moved northward, the area became less fashionable because it was out of the way. Although the surrounding neighborhood deteriorated, the houses on the park stayed in good condition until 1866—when Cornelius Vanderbilt bought the park for use as a railroad terminal. Today, the once-elegant St. John's Park is the entrance to the Holland Tunnel.

WILLIAMSBURGH. This pleasant little hamlet in Brooklyn was attractive to New York City merchants in the 1830s because of its location and convenient transportation to the city's center. At that time, real estate boomed. But by the 1840s, a large immigrant population had moved in, the area was no longer a fashionable suburb, and real estate values plummeted. It was around this time that George Stevens Schermerhorn moved his young family to 23rd Street in the upper reaches of the city's residential limits.

FIFTH AVENUE. Then a muddy, rutted road above 18th Street, by 1859 Fifth Avenue was lined with large, expensive houses. Gene reports that in 1848 most people didn't live above 8th Street. Within ten years, however, a relative of his, William Colford Schermerhorn, built a mansion at West 23rd Street on Madison Square, where his wife became one of the trend-setting leaders of society. (One frequently-reported event was a masked ball at which the guests were costumed as nobility from the court of Louis XV.)

GAMES. Marbles and kite-flying are games which predate Gene's boyhood and are still popular today. Baseball, however, was a new sport, and New York boasted the first baseball club in America—the Knickerbocker Base Ball Club of New York. Other clubs were formed, and the first game was held in New York in 1845.

PIGS. It was a complaint when New York was a Dutch settlement, and in the 1840s, pigs in the public streets were still a problem. In 1847, the Common Council (New York's city government) ordered the police to capture "any and all swine found at large within the lamp and watch districts, and to place them in the pound to be disposed of as provided in the city ordinances."

Letter No. 2

CHELSEA. The estate to which Gene refers was inherited by Clement C. Moore, remembered for his poem "A Visit from St. Nicholas" rather than his studies in the classics. His grandfather, Captain Clarke, purchased the land and built the estate, naming it after the Chelsea Royal Hospital for Old Soldiers in London. Clement Moore created streets and sold off most of the family property in 1823, donating a large section (Chelsea Square: 20th to 21st Streets between Ninth and Tenth Avenues) to the General Theological Seminary, built in 1835. The area retained the name of the original estate, and by 1846, Chelsea was growing rapidly. Clement Moore's house, described and illustrated by Gene, was demolished between

1852 and 1853 when the bluffs were leveled and the land extended into the Hudson as part of a general shoreline improvement.

FOURTH AVENUE. Above 26th Street, Fourth Avenue was considered undesirable; there were factories, tenements, saloons, and squatters' shacks. The railroad ran north from 23rd Street and was completely unfenced between 34th and 42nd Streets, making it very difficult to cross from one side of the avenue to the other. Park Avenue was not improved until the 1870s.

RUM SHOPS. There were many rum and grog shops when Gene was a boy, a pattern which began when New York was a Dutch settlement. In his 1851 book, *What I Saw in New York*, Joel Ross complained that "3,286 houses kept open for the sale of rum on the Sabbath."

ASTOR PLACE OPERA HOUSE. Located on Lafayette Street between Astor Place and 8th Street, the Opera House was of classical design, resembling a Greek temple, and was built expressly for the performance of Italian opera. The 1800-seat house was also used for drama, vaudeville, concerts, and balls. Philip Hone commented in his *Diary* on the 1843 opening of the opera house (at which he shared a box with Peter Schermerhorn): "Each owner seems to outdo the other in elegance. The scenery is beautiful. The dome and the fronts of the boxes are painted in the most superb classical designs, and the sofa-seats are exceedingly commodious. Will this splendid and refined amusement be supported in New York? I am doubtful."

In the later *Account of the Terrific and Fatal Riot at the New-York Astor Place Opera House 1849*, it was described as "fitted up and decorated with taste and magnificence, and in the opera seasons has been attended by the most wealthy and fashionable people, who have made extravagant displays of luxurious adornment. While the private boxes were taken by the season, by those who wished to enjoy the music, liked the display and could afford the expenditure, the other seats were let at a dollar admission, and the upper tier or amphitheatre was reserved for people of humbler means or more modest pretensions, at 25¢ a ticket."

ASTOR PLACE RIOT. When the Astor Place Riot occurred in 1849, its statistics (31 dead and 150 injured) made it the worst theater disaster in world history. Equally tragic were the social conditions that gave rise to the incident and were intensified by it. The overt cause was a bitter rivalry between the English tragedian, William Macready and the American, Edwin Forrest. When the management of the Astor Opera House announced Macready's forthcoming engagement, sensational newspaper headlines took advantage of the emnity between the actors and enlisted the public to choose sides. Working class groups took up the cause and posted billboards around the city exhorting working men "to express their opinion whether Americans or English should rule the city." In truth, class struggle was the basis of the riot; the Macready/Forrest affair was merely the spark that touched it off.

In nineteenth-century New York, the rich were very obviously rich, and the poor, abyssmally poor. The upper classes emulated English society, and the lower classes—mainly Irish immigrants at the time—resented those affectations. Add to this mixture the so-called Native American political parties, whose reason for existing was to oppose immigration and foreigners, and finally, the volatile street gangs whose skills were available for hire. The weeks of incitement culminated in a bloody riot at the Opera House.

Twenty thousand protesters, mainly young men, were armed with sticks and paving stones. While they agitated outside, people planted inside the theater booed Macready. The crowd in the street became angrier, the police could not control them, and the militia was sent among them, armed with bayonets and muskets. The soldiers were ordered to fire, and "there was a gleam of sulphurous light, a sharp quick rattle, and here and there in the crowd, a man sank upon the pavement with a deep groan or death rattle. . . . "

NEW YEAR'S DAY. A tradition from early Dutch New York, New Year's Day was a time to receive guests and pay calls, and it completely eclipsed Christmas as a social event. Men and children visited from house to house, greeting everyone they knew, while the women stayed home to receive the callers. In *Reminiscences of an Octogenarian* (1896), Charles Haswell wrote that on New Year's Day of 1833, he visited sixty-seven homes which were "houses in best dress, best spirits, and best looks—filling their tables with delicacies." Describing a somewhat later development, Philip Hone wrote in his *Diary* that "New Year's presents have abounded this year. This is the Parisian mode of celebrating le jour de l'an, and we are getting into it very fast. Some of the houses where I visted yesterday presented the appearance of bazaars, where rich presents were displayed, from costly cashmere shawls and silver tankards to the toy watch and child's rattle."

Letter No. 3

FRANCONI'S HIPPODROME. Built in 1853, this two-story brick building enclosed an enormous arena for circus performances and spectacles. Despite the fact that the shows were considered too daring and sensational for the period, Charles Haswell in his *Reminiscences* calls the performances "excellent," and recalls the place as a "short-lived attempt to introduce spectacular pageants, gladiatorial contests, and chariot races to New York audiences. Built . . . with brick walls and a wood and canvas roof which apparently spanned the entire enclosure without any pillars to support it, the Hippodrome seated 10,000 people." Though the opening performance attracted what the *Herald* described as a dense mass of human beings, exceeding in number any assemblage . . . ever seen inside a building in this city," the enterprise was not a financial success and was abandoned within two years.

The site itself offers a good example of the speed at which nineteenth-century New York changed; first, it held the Mildenburgher mansion, then the Franconi Hippodrome, after which followed the Madison Cottage (a tavern), and finally, the elegant Fifth Avenue Hotel (where the Prince of Wales stayed during his visit to New York).

GEORGE CHRISTY. The Christy Brothers, most prominent of the Negro Minstrels, were white men in blackface, who told jokes and sang "negro songs, sent almost daily from the south." (They weren't really brothers, either; George's last name was Harrington.) They played at Mechanics Hall for nine years. A well-known 1853 guidebook (*The Stranger's Guide Around New York and Its Vicinity*) ranked the minstrel shows among "the most select places of amusement in the city. The 'Upper Ten' can be seen here, and the silks and satins will rattle around you more than at any other place. . . . " Recalling the shows, P.T. Barnum said, "One of these that I can remember, included an actual negro, who played the bones with great skill; and indeed the rage for negro delineation very largely infected the blacks, so that eventually several companies of them were formed, which went about the country engaged in somewhat extravagant imitation of themselves." Whether Barnum was aware of the triple irony of his recollection is not entirely clear.

Letter No. 4

CHURCH OF THE HOLY COMMUNION. Unusual for this time and place, the cruciform church was designed by Richard Upjohn, more widely known as architect of Trinity Church. A progressive church in many ways, it was one of the first *not* to charge pew rental fees, and its move to 20th Street was an early prediction of the city's northward sweep. The Reverend William Muhlenberg was rector of the church and founder of St. Luke's Hospital, as well.

MURRAY HILL. This area was named after the Murray estate, a landmark during the War for Independence. At the time Gene describes, it ranged from 34th to 42nd Street between Third Avenue and Broadway.

COLORED ORPHAN ASYLUM. As may be inferred from the name of this institution, racial segregation was no stranger to nineteenth-century New York—nor were the feelings generally aligned with this practice. The association sponsoring the residence and home to be known as the Colored Orphan Asylum was formed in 1836 and raised $3,000. But, according to *Francis's Strangers Handbook for the City of New York and Brooklyn* (1857), "so great was the prejudice against that portion of the destitute whom the society proposed to relieve, that suitable premises could not be procured." In 1840, the City of New York gave a grant of twenty lots to the Society, and the institution (which looked a bit like the White House) was built on the west side of Fifth Avenue between 43rd and 44th Streets.

The building came to its end during one of the more horrifying chapters of New York history—the Draft Riots of 1863 (see glossary entry under Letter No. 9). A mob of 3,000 attacked the Colored Orphan Asylum where more than two hundred children were living with fifty matrons and attendants. As the children were taken under military escort to Blackwell's Island (today, known as Roosevelt Island), the rioters broke into the building, smashing whatever they could, throwing toys and bedding outside to burn, starting the fire that destroyed the Colored Orphan Asylum.

CRYSTAL PALACE. From the time it opened in 1853, this exhibition hall was the wonder of New York. *The Stranger's Guide Around New York and Its Vicinity* (1853) declared that the Crystal Palace, filled with treasure from all over the world, "quaint old armor from the Tower of London, Gossamer fabrics from the looms of Cashmere, Sèvres china, Gobelin tapestry . . . and a host of other works of art, will long be remembered as the most tasteful ornament that ever graced the metropolis." As Gene later remarks (Letter No. 8), the Crystal Palace burned down spectacularly in 1858, leveled within a half hour of the fire's discovery.

Letter No. 5

SNOW. Shortly after Gene observed that there was more snow when he was a boy, he experienced the blizzard of '88. Another amusing footnote to his reminiscences is the 1846 guidebook entry stating that in New York, winter lasts only two months—January and February—and gardening usually begins by early March. Choose the point of view you prefer.

SLEIGH RIDING. Gene enjoyed the noisy excitement of riding the public sleigh with friends and strangers alike, all the way down Broadway to the South Ferry (the present route of the M-6 bus). Another childhood account of sleigh riding can be found in ten-year-old Catherine Havens' diary (1849–1850). No less enthusiastic, her description underscores the difference in upbringing for girls and boys of their class. The rules of deportment for young girls would not have allowed Catherine to ride the public sleigh unaccompanied by an adult, but when there was good snow, a sleigh was hired just for Catherine and her schoolmates for a ride down Broadway to the Battery and back. Her sleigh was "open and very long; and has long seats on each side, and straw on the floor to keep our feet warm, and the sleigh bells sound so cheerful."

Since childhood outings and fond memories of them generate their own magic, it is only fair to examine another point of view. Far from being a wide-eyed child, George Templeton Strong was a fairly cantankerous adult who kept a diary from 1835 to 1875, and his observations on sleigh riding were markedly different from either Gene's or Catherine's:

> These insane vehicles carry each its hundred sufferers, of whom about half have to stand in the wet straw with their feet freezing and occasionally stamped on by their fellow travelers, their ears and noses tingling in the bitter wind, their hats always on the point of being blown off. When the chariot stops, they tumble forward and when it starts again, they tumble backward, and when they arrive at the end of their ride, they commonly land up to their knees in a snowdrift, through which they flounder as best they may, to escape the little fast trotting vehicles that are coming straight at them. Many of the cross streets are still untraveled by anything on wheels or runners, but in Broadway, the Bowery and any other great thoroughfares, there is an organism of locomotion. It's more than a carnival; it's a wintry dionysiaca.

MOCK AUCTION ROOMS. Contemporary guides and news accounts warned the unsuspecting of these shady enterprises. From *The Stranger's Guide Around New York* (1853): "In almost every newspaper in New York but every few days accounts are published of some green country genius, who has bought a real gold, patent lever, full-jeweled watch, warranted, for only $15, and asked in the back room to settle, when he is swindled out of every dollar he has about him. The piratical flags of these bold buccaneers can be seen flying on almost every block in the lower part of Broadway and Chatham Street. The shops have 4 or 5 persons inside with a flag 'Great sale of gold watches: $18 per ounce paid for California gold dust &C'."

Letter No. 6

MECHANICS SOCIETY SCHOOL. There were a number of technical institutions in nineteenth-century New York, and this was the oldest, founded in 1820. Gene attended the school with several hundred other pupils, mainly the sons of merchants and apprentices. The Mechanics Society School offered courses in book-keeping, writing, drawing, architecture, science, and mechanics, and by 1855, it opened an evening division.

SHOT TOWER. Gene's memory was a bit off this time, for the tower he remembered being at 51st Street and the East River, was actually at the foot of 53rd Street. Built in 1821 to replace one which had been destroyed during the War for Independence, this tower was used to make ammunition during the Civil War. The manufacturing process was to pour molten lead through a strainer at the top of the very high tower. As the lead dropped, it formed pellets, and at the bottom of the tower, the pellets (or shot) fell into a pool of water which cooled and hardened them.

LATTING OBSERVATORY. It was an impressive structure with an overall height of 350 feet, and *Francis's Strangers Handbook* (1857) assures, "It is not inappropriate to remark that the building is quite safe, having been carefully examined by scientific men who have made a favorable report. It stands on 43rd Street, the entrance being from 42nd through a building 125 feet long. On either side of the passage is a continuous bazaar. In the upper story is an ice-cream saloon elegantly fitted up for ladies. The tower is an octagon, 75 feet in diameter at the base, with an extreme height of 350 feet. It is of timber, well braced with iron, and is anchored at each of the 8 angles with about 40 tons of stone and timber."

Letter No. 7

VOLUNTEER FIRE DEPARTMENT. In 1853, the department comprised 34 engine companies, 49 hose companies, 8 hook and ladder companies, and more than 2,000 men, each with great pride in his own company. This pride was responsible for an equally great rivalry between companies which sometimes led to violence. The volunteers encompassed all social strata from a Livingston or Schermerhorn to a Bowery Boy, or gang member, and their common purpose united them. There was no pay for their service, but firemen were exempt from jury duty and military service for five years.

MOSE, THE BOWERY BOY. Old Mose Humphries was said to be enormous and have the strength of ten men. As a fire fighter, he was revered as a hero—and away from the department, he was renowned for his prowess as a street fighter. In illustrations, he is generally shown leaning against a fire hydrant or plug, guarding it for his company; rival companies would often battle as fiercely to control the fireplug as they would to control the fire.

In the 1840s, Mose led the Bowery Boys (one of the most infamous gangs of the period) in fights against enemy gangs—the Dead Rabbit and the Plug Uglies. Street gangs continued to be a part of nineteenth-century New York life, and in fact, were a major force in the Astor Place and Draft Riots; their battle cry was Mose's name. By 1849 he was something of a folk hero, and a play with a character modeled after him had a long run at the Olympic Theater.

Letter No. 8

SUNFISH POND. The pond Gene remembers is not Sunfish Pond, which was located between 31st and 33rd Streets and Madison and Lexington Avenues. Similar to the network of ponds and streams that Gene describes as starting uptown in the 60s and eventually emptying into Turtle Bay, the stream which was the source of the real Sunfish Pond meandered much the same way in the low 30s from Broadway, east to Kip's Bay. Sunfish Pond was a prime hunting and fishing spot for boys (Gene's father among them, most likely), a good skating rink in the winter, and an excellent source of water to put out serious fires. Eventually, it was destroyed as a fish pond, contaminated by Peter Cooper's glue factory. Because of New York's continuing expansion and need for land, Sunfish Pond was drained and filled in 1839.

BLOOMINGDALE. The Bloomingdale Road was the name for the upper part of Broadway. Opened in 1703, it extended from 23rd to 114th Street, and in 1795, was open all the way to 147th Street. The lovely suburb, named for a Dutch town meaning "Vale of Flowers," centered around 100th Street and the Bloomingdale Road, and numbered among its notable residences the Apthorp Mansion, between 91st and 92nd Streets, west of what is now Columbus Avenue, and the Striker's Bay Mansion, at 96th Street. Edgar Allan Poe was a Bloomingdale resident for a time, boarding at a cottage just off the road at 84th Street. There, in 1845, he wrote "The Raven."

FERNANDO WOOD. Mayor of New York from 1854 to 1859, he later became a representative to Congress. In 1861, he recommended that New York secede from the state and become a free city.

UPPER WEST SIDE. West End Avenue, Riverside Park and Drive were not developed until the late 1880s when Riverside Drive was expected to become Millionaire's Row.

Letter No. 9

SEVENTH REGIMENT. This distinguished regiment was made up of bankers' and brokers' sons and the rest of New York's aristocracy. As indicated at various points in this book, the Schermerhorns were traditionally active in the Seventh, culminating with Edward Gibert Schermerhorn (Phil's brother), a major, active in the military throughout his life.

DRAFT RIOTS. In July 1863 occurred one of the worst episodes in New York City's history, and as in the Astor Place Riot, class conflict played its part.

The Civil War was on and Congress had passed a conscription act—with an escape clause for those with means. Under the regulations of the act, a young man could legally avoid military service by paying $300 for a substitute. This was a tremendous sum of money at the time, and understandably, the conscription act and the people wealthy enough to benefit from it were mightily resented. What is less understandable—in terms of logic let alone humanity—is that the wrath of the (white) lower classes was redirected at the only group less powerful than they were: the blacks. Said to be incited by Confederate agents and Southern sympathizers, the poor whites went on a rampage: Why should they go to war and risk death to free slaves—when these same slaves might come north and take away their jobs? Rabble rousers agitated, the mob was seeded with bands of trained, armed thugs, and the black people of New York were under total seige—tortured, mutilated, and lynched (and those whites who tried to help or bury victims received the same treatment). After five days, the rioting was brought under control by the militia.

Letter No. 10

JONES' WOODS. In response to those who criticized the Commissioner's Plan of 1811, saying that inadequate land was set aside for parks and squares, Jones' Woods was seriously considered as a site for the Great Park before the location for Central Park was chosen. Jones' Woods was forest untouched since the beginning of time, until it was divided into lots and sold by the City of New York.

YORKVILLE. This separate village on the Old Post Road, extending from 83rd to 89th Street and from Fourth to Second Avenue, became a German settlement in the early 1900s. A community of German immigrants, living around St. Mark's Place, relocated in the village of Yorkville after the *General Slocum* excursion boat horror. The traumatic event occurred on a summer Sunday afternoon. The boat caught fire; the captain and crew panicked, taking the boat farther away from the shore, and many German family members (mostly women and children) died in sight of the shore and just beyond help.

HARLEM. *The Stranger's Guide Around New York* (1853) described Harlem as being "situated south-east of Manhattanville, on Harlem River, near its discharge into Long Island Sound. It is a flourishing village, with several churches, and a super-abundance of hotels, besides a commodious depot, belonging to the New-York and Harlem Railroad Company. The cars for Harlem start every hour from the depot, north-east of the City Hall. Distance, 7 miles."

An early Dutch settlement from the days of Peter Stuyvesant, Harlem was an area of large farms. Although various ethnic groups have lived there, Harlem, throughout much of the twentieth century, has been regarded as both center of black culture and ghetto. In fact, black people, though not in the majority, lived there from the seventeenth century onward as slaves on the farms and estates; the 1790 census listed "115 slaves for the Harlem division, just under one-third of its total population." (*Daily Advertiser* [New York], January 15, 1791)

Index to Historical Glossary

Note: The number in parentheses indicates the letter in which the entry appears; the following number is the page where the term is discussed in the glossary.

Bibliography

Churchill, Allen. THE UPPER CRUST. An Informal History of New York's Highest Society. New Jersey, Prentice-Hall, 1970.

Dunshee, Kenneth Holcomb. AS YOU PASS BY. New York, Hastings House, 1952.

Ellis, Edward Robb. THE EPIC OF NEW YORK CITY. New York, Coward-McCann, 1966.

FRANCIS'S STRANGERS HANDBOOK FOR THE CITY OF NEW YORK AND BROOKLYN AND THE VICINITY. New York, C.S. Francis, 1857.

Hamm, Margherita-Arlina. FAMOUS FAMILIES OF NEW YORK. New York, Heraldic Publishing Co, 1970 (Reprint of 1901 edition)

Haswell, Charles. REMINISCENCES OF AN OCTOGENARIAN IN THE CITY OF NEW YORK (1816–1860). New York, Harper, 1896.

Havens, Catherine Elizabeth. DIARY OF A LITTLE GIRL IN OLD NEW YORK. New York, Henry Collins Brown, 1919.

Hone, Philip. THE DIARY OF PHILIP HONE 1828–1852. 2 vol. Allan Nevins, ed. New York, Dodd, Mead & Co., 1927.

Kelley, Frank Bergen. HISTORICAL GUIDE TO THE CITY OF NEW YORK. New York, Frederick A. Stokes, 1909.

Lockwood, Charles. MANHATTAN MOVES UPTOWN, Boston, Houghton Mifflin, 1976.

_____BRICKS AND BROWNSTONE. The New York Row House, 1783–1929. An Architectural and Social History. New York, McGraw-Hill, 1972.

Mott, Hopper Striker. THE NEW YORK OF YESTERDAY: A Descriptive Narrative of Old Bloomingdale. New York, Putnam, 1908.

Ross, Joel. WHAT I SAW IN NEW YORK; Or, A Bird's Eye View of the City Life. Auburn, NY, Derby & Miller, 1851.

Schermerhorn, Richard. SCHERMERHORN GENEALOGY AND FAMILY CHRONICLE. New York, Tobias A. Wright, 1914.

Scoville, Joseph (Walter Barrett, pseudonym) THE OLD MERCHANTS OF NEW YORK. New York, Carleton, 1866.

Sheldon, George W. THE STORY OF THE VOLUNTEER FIRE DEPARTMENT OF THE CITY OF NEW YORK. New York, Harper & Bros, 1882.

Stokes, I.N. Phelps. THE ICONOGRAPHY OF MANHATTAN ISLAND. 1498–1909. New York, Robert H. Dodd, 1928.

STRANGER'S GUIDE AROUND NEW YORK AND ITS VICINITY. What to See and What is to be Seen with Hints and Advice to Those Who Visit the Great Metropolis. New York, Graham, 1853.

Strong, George Templeton. THE DIARY OF GEORGE TEMPLETON STRONG. 1835–1875 Allan Nevins and Milton Halsey Thomas, eds. 4 vol. New York, Macmillan, 1952.

November 16th, 1888

From 63rd to 80th St. and from 3rd Ave.
to the river was a beautiful piece
of woodland with hills and dales
brooks and noble old Trees. It belonged to the Jones' and Schermerhorn,
and was known as "Jones' Woods". It
was a favorite place for Picnics and
Excursions.

"Hell Gate" Ferry at the foot of 86th St.

Yorkville was a small village with its
centre about 3rd Avenue and 86th Street
and spreading a few blocks each way

Above 92nd St. Harlem Commons began.
This was the low land extending from
the East River at 90th St to the Hudson
at 124th St (Manhattanville). It was
cut up into farms and intersected by
creeks running in from both rivers
At 109th St and 2nd Ave was the "Red
House" a road house with a race
track and beer garden.
Harlem was like another village.
extending from 125th St along the 2nd
3rd and 4th Avenues to the Harlem
River.

"Harlem Bridge at the end of
Third Avenue
Other bridges crossed the river at 4th
Avenue (Railroad), 8th Ave (McComb Dam)

and Kings Bridge on the line of
the Bloomingdale Road.
High Bridge could only be reached
by a long drive or by boat.

Now my dear Phil I have tried
to tell you what this great city
was like when I was a boy but
little older than yourself, and I
hope I have succeeded in interesting
you somewhat; I have begun with
my earliest recollections of New
York and I will leave it now
about 1836 when the population
was only 629,810 - less than half
what it was at the last census in
1880, It is estimated now at over
1,500,000, I cannot help looking
forward and wondering, if it can
possibly be that you can tell of as
great changes, It is my firm belief
that you will be able to do so and
that you will live to see the entire
island as thickly built as it is

now below 59th St and perhaps the
district above the Harlem also, Or
it may be that you will see changes
that I don't even dream of, although
my faith in the future of New York
is unbounded, I could go on and
write many more letters, telling of
things which I have hinted at and
of interesting events of a later date,
I have preferred to stop here in my
story which perhaps has not been very
interesting after all— and yet I hope
you will sometimes enjoy reading what
has given me so much pleasure to
write for you

               Your loving
                   Uncle Irne

Goudy Old Style and Zapf Chancery are the typefaces used for text and display, respectively. Eighty-pound Mohawk ivory vellum is the stock, and the printing was done by Haddon Craftsmen, Inc., Scranton, Pennsylvania.